P9-CEL-842

THE FIFTH

Garfield

TREASURY

THE FIFTH

Garfield

TREASURY

BY: JIM DAVIS

BALLANTINE BOOKS • NEW YORK

Copyright © 1989 United Feature Syndicate, Inc.

The Sunday strips appearing here in color were previously included in black
and white in *GARFIELD Worldwide, GARFIELD Rounds Out,* and *GARFIELD
Chews the Fat.*

All rights reserved under International and Pan-American Copyright
Conventions. Published in the United States by Ballantine Books, a division of
Random House, Inc., New York, and simultaneously in Canada by Random
House of Canada Limited, Toronto, Canada

Library of Congress Catalog Card Number: 88-92857

ISBN: 0-345-36268-3

First Edition: November 1989

10 9 8 7 6 5 4 3 2 1

What's the difference between a skinny person and a stick? A dog has to work harder to fetch a skinny person.

Why is it smart to take skinny people along when you go camping?

BECAUSE YOU CAN ALWAYS RUB THEM TOGETHER TO START A FIRE.

GARFIELD'S FAVORITE SKINNY JOKES

What do skinny people do for fun?

They like to count their ribs.

HOW MANY SKINNY PEOPLE DOES IT TAKE TO EAT A SUNDAE?

5 ONE TO EAT THE SUNDAE AND FOUR TO SHARE THE GUILT.

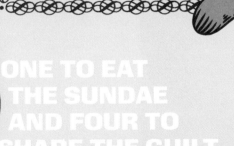

What do you call a skinny person who gains weight?

CURED!

Why is it dangerous for skinny people to jog? They keep falling through the cracks in the sidewalk.

I once knew a guy who was so skinny, the first time he went out, somebody tried to hang a flag from him.

© 1986 United Feature Syndicate, Inc.

© 1986 United Feature Syndicate, Inc.

JIM DAVIS 12-7

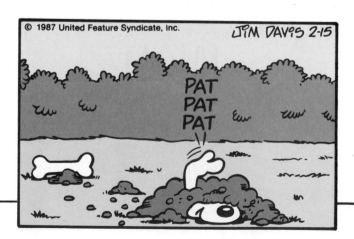

© 1987 United Feature Syndicate, Inc.

JiM DAViS 2-15

© 1987 United Feature Syndicate, Inc.

© 1987 United Feature Syndicate, Inc.

© 1987 United Feature Syndicate, Inc.

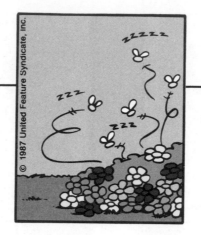

© 1987 United Feature Syndicate, Inc.

JIM DAVIS 5-31

© 1987 United Feature Syndicate, Inc.

© 1987 United Feature Syndicate, Inc.

6-21

JIM DAVIS

© 1987 United Feature Syndicate, Inc.

© 1987 United Feature Syndicate, Inc.

© 1987 United Feature Syndicate, Inc.

YANK

WHIRRRR

WHIRRRR

JIM DAVIS 8-30

© 1987 United Feature Syndicate, Inc. JiM DAViS 9-20

© 1987 United Feature Syndicate, Inc.

© 1987 United Feature Syndicate, Inc.

© 1987 United Feature Syndicate, Inc.

© 1987 United Feature Syndicate, Inc.   JIM DAVIS 1-3-88

1988 United Feature Syndicate, Inc.

© 1988 United Feature Syndicate, Inc.

© 1988 United Feature Syndicate, Inc.

© 1988 United Feature Syndicate, Inc.

© 1988 United Feature Syndicate, Inc.

JiM DAViS 6-12

HAPPY 10TH BIRTHDAY, BUDDY, JIM DAVIS

© 1988 United Feature Syndicate, Inc.

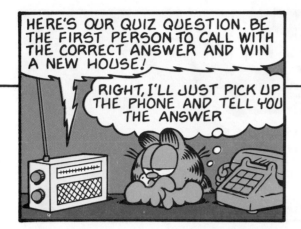

© 1988 United Feature Syndicate, Inc.

TELL YOU WHAT, GARFIELD. IF I GIVE YOU ONE OF MY HAMBURGERS, WILL YOU STOP STARING AT ME?

AGREED!

© 1988 United Feature Syndicate, Inc.

JIM DAVIS 8-14

9-25

© 1988 United Feature Syndicate, Inc.

JIM DAVIS

ZIP!

ZIP!

© 1988 United Feature Syndicate, Inc.

GOOD MORNING, GARFIELD

11-6

© 1988 United Feature Syndicate, Inc.

© 1988 United Feature Syndicate, Inc.

© 1988 United Feature Syndicate, Inc.

Garfield's Sleeping Tips

1 Be adventurous. Anyone can sleep in a bed. But a true genius might prefer a bathtub filled with gerbils.

2
1. CLOSE EYES.
2. OPEN EYES.
3. SMASH ALARM CLOCK.
4. REPEAT STEP ONE.

3 *Counting sheep does not make you sleepy; it makes you a shepherd.*

8
GET A TEDDY BEAR
Preferably one that doesn't snore.

Sleeping is an art. Here are some tips to help you create a snoozy masterpiece:

4 Midnight snacks keep you awake. Stuff yourself at 11:30.

5 *If they think you're in a coma, you're doing it right.*

7 You know it's bedtime when you start reading with your face.

6 Pay no attention to those noises under the bed.

9 If you toss and turn all night, you may have fallen asleep in a clothes dryer.

10 *You sleep better if someone you love is close by.*

STRIPS, SPECIALS OR BESTSELLING BOOKS. . .
GARFIELD'S ON EVERYONE'S MENU

Don't miss even one episode in the Tubby Tabby's hilarious series!

__GARFIELD AT LARGE (#1)   32013-1/$6.95
__GARFIELD GAINS WEIGHT (#2)   32008-5/$6.95
__GARFIELD BIGGER THAN LIFE (#3)   32007-7/$6.95
__GARFIELD WEIGHS IN (#4)   32010-7/$6.95
__GARFIELD TAKES THE CAKE (#5))   32009-3/$6.95
__GARFIELD EATS HIS HEART OUT (#6)   32018-2/$6.95
__GARFIELD SITS AROUND THE HOUSE (#7)   32011-5/$6.95
__GARFIELD TIPS THE SCALES (#8)   33580-5/$6.95
__GARFIELD LOSES HIS FEET (#9)   31805-6/$6.95
__GARFIELD MAKE IT BIG (#10)   31928-1/$6.95
__GARFIELD ROLLS ON (#11)   32634-2/$6.95
__GARFIELD OUT TO LUNCH (#12)   33118-4/$6.95
__GARFIELD FOOD FOR THOUGHT(#13)   34129-5/$6.95

__GARFIELD SWALLOWS HIS PRIDE (#14)   34725-0/$6.95
__GARFIELD WORLDWIDE (#15)   35158-2/$6.95
__GARFIELD ROUNDS OUT (#16)   35388-9/$6.95
__GARFIELD CHEWS THE FAT (#17)   35956-9/$6.95

GARFIELD AT HIS SUNDAY BEST!
__GARFIELD TREASURY   33106-5/$8.95
__THE SECOND GARFIELD TREASURY   33276-8/$8.95
__THE THIRD GARFIELD TREASURY   32635-0/$8.95
__THE FOURTH GARFIELD TREASURY   34726-9/$9.95
__THE FIFTH GARFIELD TREASURY   36268-3/$9.95

BALLANTINE SALES
Dept. TA, 201 E. 50th St., New York, N.Y. 10022

Please send me the BALLANTINE or DEL REY BOOKS I have checked above. I am enclosing $ .... (add .75 per copy to cover postage and handling). Send check or money order—no cash or C.O.D.'s please. Prices and numbers are subject to change without notice.

Name _____

Address _____

City_____ State_____ Zip Code_____

30   Allow at least 4 weeks for delivery   TA-135